**DATE DUE**

*Explorers & Exploration*

# The Travels of
# Juan Ponce de León

**By Deborah Crisfield**
**Illustrated by Patrick O'Brien**

Raintree Steck-Vaughn Publishers

A Harcourt Company

Austin · New York
www.steck-vaughn.com

Published by Raintree Steck-Vaughn Publishers, an imprint of Steck-Vaughn Company


**Library of Congress Cataloging-in-Publication Data**
Crisfield, Deborah.
    Juan Ponce de Leon/by Deborah Crisfield.
        p. cm. — (Explorers and exploration)
        ISBN 0-7398-1491-5
        1. Ponce de León, Juan, 1460?–1521—Juvenile literature
2. Explorers—America—Biography—Juvenile literature   3. Explorers—
Spain—Biography—Juvenile literature   4. America—Discovery and
exploration—Spanish—Juvenile literature   [1. Ponce de León, Juan,
1460?–1521. 2. Explorers. 3. America—Discovery and exploration—
Spanish.]
    I. Title. II. Series.

E125.P7 C75 2001
970.01'6'092—dc21                                00-041942

Printed and bound in the United States of America
10 9 8 7 6 5 4 3 2 1 W 02 01 00

Produced by By George Productions, Inc.

Illustration Acknowledgments:
pp 5, 19, 21, 29, 31, 35, 38, and 41, The New York Public Library; pp 7, 8, 13, and 37, North Wind Picture Archives.
All other artwork and maps are by Patrick O'Brien.

# Contents

# The Early Years

If you were the son of a Spanish nobleman in the 1400s, you did not have many choices about what you could do when you grew up. If you were the oldest son, you would inherit, or receive, your father's property when he died. If you were a younger son, you would learn to become a soldier. Because he was a younger son, a young Spanish boy named Juan Ponce de León became a soldier. At the time, no one had any idea that this would lead to him being the first European to reach the land that is now called Florida.

For a man who would later have pages and pages written about his life, there is very little known about Ponce de León's early years. Juan was most likely born in a town called Santervás de Campos in Spain. The year was probably 1474.

As a young boy, Juan went to work as a page for a nobleman named Don Pedro Núñez de Guzman.

**Ponce de León**

Although a page was a servant, the job prepared the boy for war. In addition to the work the page had to do, he was given lessons in the art of war. When a nobleman thought a page was ready, he made the boy a squire. As a squire, the boy had more lessons and less work.

Both of these jobs were considered a privilege and were only offered to sons of noblemen. The noblemen would send their sons to one another's homes, because they did not think a boy should be a servant in his own home.

Juan learned his lessons well—both as a page and later as a squire. He probably saw quite a bit of action, first as a squire and later as a soldier, during the last years of the war between the Spanish and the Moors. The Moors were a group of people who were originally from North Africa. Hundreds of years before, they had invaded Spain. Ever since, the Spanish had been trying to force them out. The Spanish saw the Moors as intruders. They also disliked them because they were Muslims, followers of the prophet Muhammad. They were not Christians as the king and queen of Spain had declared everyone must be.

**Ponce de León saw much fighting during his youth.**

The war between the Christian Spaniards and the Muslim Moors was a major part of life in Spain at that time. No one could remember when there hadn't been fighting. But at the end of the 15th century, the Moors were driven out of Spain.

Spain's victory was welcomed, but suddenly most of the country's young men were out of work. If they weren't first-born sons, they had no land. If there was no war, they had no job. Like lots of young soldiers, 18-year-old Juan suddenly found himself faced with an uncertain future.

Things changed quickly, however, when Christopher Columbus returned to Spain. The explorer brought amazing news with him. There was new, uncharted land across the ocean. And men trained in battle were needed to settle it. Columbus intended to return there as soon as possible.

Going to this unexplored land, which Europeans began calling the New World, suited Ponce de León perfectly. He was an adventurous young man, skilled in fighting. He had few reasons to stay in Spain, and very little money.

The unexplored land across the ocean offered him both the chance for excitement and the chance to become rich. Juan jumped at the opportunity. Many other young Spaniards wanted to sail with Columbus. Because Juan Ponce de León had made a name for himself fighting the Moors, he earned a spot on Columbus's second voyage. The year was 1493, and Juan was 19 years old.

Ponce de León sailed with Columbus on
his second voyage to the Americas.

# Off to the New World

**C**olumbus had discovered several islands on his last trip, and he named the largest one Hispaniola. This was where the first Spanish colony was going to be established. A colony is an area that has been settled by people from another country, and is governed by that country.

More than 2,000 people went with Columbus on this second trip. There were soldiers, carpenters, farmers, tradespeople, priests, merchants, and even some women. Many people with different kinds of skills were needed to set up a permanent, or lasting, colony. Ponce de León went as a soldier.

The island of Hispaniola was populated by a tribe of native people called the Taino. They were part of a large group of native inhabitants called the Arawak. On the previous trip, Columbus saw that they were a peaceful and generous people. They were more than happy to trade with the Europeans and show them the riches of the land.

To Columbus, the Taino's behavior meant it would be easy for him and his men to force the natives to work for them. Not surprisingly, the natives did not like this. Ponce de León's job as a soldier was to make them obey—or kill them.

There is very little record of Ponce de León during his first eight years on Hispaniola. But it is known that by 1502 he was in charge of all the troops on the eastern half of the island. He also married a Spanish woman during that time, and they had three daughters and a son.

**A native house on Hispaniola**

By 1504 most of the native people had been killed or made to work for the Spaniards. Some, however, still fought back. These natives lived in the section of the island known as Higuey. The governor of Hispaniola, Nicolás de Ovando, decided that Ponce de León was the man to lead the Spanish forces against them.

Ponce de León succeeded in overcoming the Taino. In fact, he was so successful that Ovando put him in command of Higuey. Ponce de León moved his family there and built a huge stone house for them. This was unusual. Most Spaniards built temporary houses out of mud, straw, and wood. They only wanted to make their fortunes and return to Spain. Ponce de León, on the other hand, was obviously planning to make his home there last forever.

**Europeans brought many new diseases to the island of Hispaniola.**

When the Spanish settlers came to the island, they had brought lots of new diseases with them. Because the native peoples had never had these diseases, their bodies were not able to fight them. Many of them died from illness. Thousands of others were killed by the Spanish soldiers. No one is sure of the exact numbers, but some experts think there may have been as many as 8 million natives on the island when Columbus first landed there. Twenty years later, there were fewer than 30,000. Twenty years after that, there would be just a few hundred left.

# Puerto Rico

The island of Hispaniola was very close
to another island that the native people called
Borinquen. Before the Spaniards arrived,
the natives of the two islands had traded with
one another, since they were both part of the
Taino tribe.

The natives of Hispaniola were full of stories
of the island of Borinquen, and word soon spread
among the Spaniards that the neighboring land
was full of gold. Soon the Spanish were calling the
island the "rich port," or in Spanish, *puerto rico.*

When Ovando learned of the *puerto rico,* he
decided to conquer Borinquen. Juan Ponce de
León led the forces. In 1506 Ponce de León set
off with five fast sailing ships called caravels. This
first trip was just to explore the island. There were
no plans to settle it yet.

Borinquen proved to be everything it was
supposed to be. Not only was there much gold,
but the natives were friendly and helpful. Ponce
de León returned to Ovando with a glowing
report of the island.

After a lot of bargaining with the king of Spain and Ovando, Ponce de León was made the governor of Borinquen. A governor is the person who rules an area. Ponce de León returned there with more men and started a settlement. He moved his family there, built a new stone house, dug for gold, and soon became very rich. Many other settlers joined him on the island as word of the riches spread.

Just as they had done on Hispaniola, the Spanish forced the natives to work for them and killed them if they didn't. After five years of this, the native peoples of Borinquen began to fight back, just as the natives of Hispaniola had done. Ponce de León organized the Spanish forces against them and once again defeated the natives.

Hundreds of thousands of natives occupied the island before the Spaniards arrived. Only 4,000 were left ten years later.

**Spanish caravels sailed to Borinquen (now Puerto Rico) to conquer the island and its people.**

# The Fountain of Youth

**P**once de León did not get to enjoy being governor of Borinquen for very long. When King Ferdinand and Queen Isabella paid for Columbus's voyage in 1492, they signed an agreement saying that Columbus and his children would be the governors of all the new places he came to. Columbus's son, Diego, was able to prove that his father had landed on Borinquen before Ponce de León. In 1512 Diego Columbus won the right to be its governor.

Now that Diego Columbus was ruler of the island, Ponce de León did not want to stay there. He went to King Ferdinand and asked to be

**Ponce de León searching for the Fountain of Youth**

allowed to explore other islands. He had three good reasons why he should do this. First, the king owed him something for taking away his title. Second, Spain would have the glory of gaining new lands. Third, and perhaps most appealing to the aging king, there were rumors of an island that had powerful healing waters: the Fountain of Youth!

The natives on both Borinquen and Hispaniola spoke of a special water on an island called Bimini. Bathing in the water could cure sickness. And if anyone drank it, he or she would become young again and stay young forever. The Fountain of Youth would be appealing to anyone, but especially to 60-year-old King Ferdinand.

There is no written record that the king ordered Ponce de León to search for these magical waters. Instead, the record shows that the purpose of the trip was to discover new lands and riches for Spain and to convert the natives to Catholicism. But through word of mouth, the rumor spread that Juan Ponce de León was off on a search for the Fountain of Youth.

**Many people drew pictures of what they thought had happened during Ponce de León's search for the Fountain of Youth.**

Ponce de León became the first known European
to land in Florida.

# A Trip of Discovery

**P**once de León set out to explore new lands on March 3, 1513. He had three ships and about 60 people with him. They headed northwest, in the direction that Bimini was supposed to lie. Roughly one month later, around Easter, the Spaniards did find land. It wasn't on any of their maps. Ponce de León claimed this land for Spain.

It soon became clear that this land was probably not Bimini. There were no natives to be found, and no Fountain of Youth. The land, however, was beautiful. It was dense with trees, flowers, and other plant life. Ponce de León named it Florida. The word *florida* is Spanish for "flowery." It was the perfect name for the flowery land that Ponce de León first saw on Easter Sunday.

Ponce de León thought that Florida was another island. He had no idea that he had just come to a continent. He also wasn't sure if any people lived there. He took his ships south along the coast to see if he could find any signs of human life.

During this journey southward, he made a discovery. His ships were fighting against a powerful current. A current is a stream of water that flows very fast and strong. This current is now known as the Gulf Stream. Just as he didn't realize that Florida was a continent, Ponce de León didn't realize how useful the Gulf Stream would be to sailors traveling to Europe.

The Gulf Stream is like a river in the Atlantic Ocean. It flows northward along Florida's east coast up to North Carolina. Then it heads east to Europe. Ponce de León's ships were sailing against it. All of the ships' sails were full of wind, yet the ships were barely moving forward. In fact, at one point, Ponce de León thought they might even be heading backward. The sailors dropped the anchors to see if that would hold them. The anchors held two ships, but one was pulled away by the powerful current. The Spaniards did not see the missing ship again for two days.

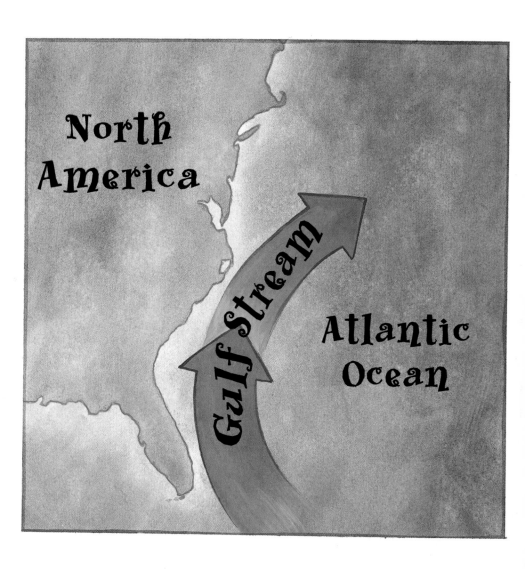

**A map showing the Gulf Stream**

Ponce de León and the remaining ship's captain, Antonio Alaminos, were able to sail southward again once they found that the ships could move out of the Gulf Stream.

Even though he was the first to discover the Gulf Stream, Ponce de León never realized how important it was. The other captain did, however. Many years later Alaminos mapped out the Gulf Stream to create a much faster trade route back to Europe.

# Meeting with the Natives

There was no time to think about the strange ocean current. Native people appeared on the beach while the two ships were anchored offshore. They seemed eager to welcome the explorers to their land and waved for them to come in closer. As the Spaniards approached, however, the natives attacked them. Ponce de León and his men quickly returned to the ships and sailed southward once again.

At one point, the Spaniards anchored and went ashore at an area that looked deserted. They needed to wait for their missing ship, and to get more water. However, it was not long before they were attacked again.

These natives were from the Ais tribe. Most likely they were from the same tribe that had attacked the Spaniards before.

**Native people attacking Ponce de León**

There is no record of the Ais having ever met Europeans before. However, experts think that because they began to fight with the Spaniards as soon as they saw them, they already may have had some experience with other Europeans. This time, the Spaniards fought back. Then they headed south and around the tip of Florida.

As they rounded the tip, they came upon a series of small islands that together are now known as the Florida Keys. There they met native people who said they had gold and were willing to trade. One of them even spoke Spanish. This was a big surprise. Because Florida was not on any map, it would seem that no one from Europe had been there before. But since this native spoke Spanish, perhaps someone from Spain had come here earlier.

Ponce de León and his crew never figured out how this person had learned to speak Spanish, but they were grateful for it. Since the Spaniards were eager to trade with these people, it would be useful to be able to talk with them. Good feelings quickly turned to bad, though, when the two groups couldn't agree. The natives tried to seize a ship.

Ponce de León and his men fought back. They captured four women, who they hoped would help them in their dealings with the other natives.

The prisoners told the Spaniards of a group of natives up north who had lots of gold to trade. Hearing this, Ponce de León turned the ships northward up the west coast of Florida.

The Spaniards found the natives, but these people too attacked them. Now Ponce de León turned his ships toward home.

**Some experts believe that Ponce de León searched for the Fountain of Youth for more than a year.**

# Fighting the Caribs

On his way home, Juan Ponce de León came to more islands, including the ones now called the Tortugas, the Bahamas, and Cuba. He told Alaminos to continue the search for Bimini. (Alaminos later found an island with that name in the Caribbean, but there was no Fountain of Youth on it.) Ponce de León sailed on to Borinquen and arrived there in October 1513. From there he headed back to Spain to report to the king.

# MAP OF PONCE DE LEÓN'S VOYAGE

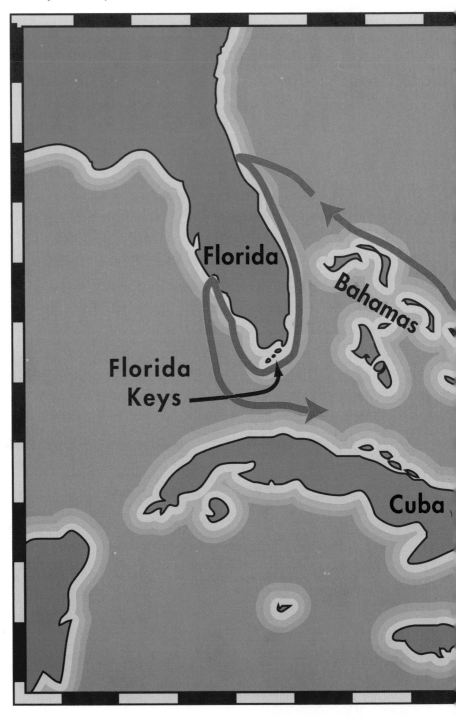

Florida

Bahamas

Florida
Keys

Cuba

CARIBBEAN
SEA

Hispaniola

Puerto
Rico

Ponce de León arrived in Spain in spring 1514. Not surprisingly, King Ferdinand was thrilled when he heard about Florida, even without the Fountain of Youth. He made Ponce de León governor of Florida and ordered him to return there to settle it. The explorer was more than happy to do this. Unfortunately, he couldn't get back to Florida as quickly as he hoped.

Ponce de León was asked to lead a Spanish force against the Caribs. They were a native tribe that lived on islands near Borinquen and Hispaniola. The Caribs often attacked the Spanish settlers, and now the Spaniards decided that they must be stopped once and for all. It took several years, but eventually Ponce de León defeated the Carib tribe.

Even after Ponce de León defeated the Caribs, he couldn't sail off for Florida immediately. While the explorer was fighting the native people, King Ferdinand had died. Ponce de León had to go back to Spain to make sure that everything the king had promised him was still going to be honored.

Ponce de León stayed in Spain for two years this time. Eventually he was ready to sail home to Borinquen, knowing that Florida was his to settle.

**Spanish explorers were very cruel to the native peoples of the Caribbean Islands.**

# The Final Voyage of Ponce de León

Finally, Juan Ponce de León sailed for Florida in February 1521. He had only two ships this time, but many more people. His plan was to conquer and settle, not just to explore, Florida. He filled his ships with soldiers, settlers, and craftspeople for this purpose.

Ponce de León took his ships up the west coast of Florida. He chose a deserted spot and began to build a fort. Before the fort was completed, however, a native tribe called the Calusa attacked.

During a battle, Ponce de León received an arrow wound in the thigh. The wound quickly became infected. In the 1500s there was very little medicine. An infection frequently led to death. This was the reason why a fountain with magical healing powers was so appealing to people of this time.

A wounded Ponce de León is carried to his ship.

Ponce de León's arrow wound became infected.

Ponce de León knew his only chance of survival was to get to a Spanish settlement. He sailed for Cuba. Unfortunately, it was already too late. The infected wound got worse, and in July 1521 Juan Ponce de León died.

Spain had lost one of its best soldiers. Ponce de León was in his late forties when he died. The man who is remembered for his search for the Fountain of Youth did not live into old age.

Ponce de León's search for the magical waters was a complete failure—if he was looking for it in the first place. (There is no evidence that proves he was.) Also, he never realized that Florida was not an island, but part of a continent. In addition, he probably was not the first Spaniard there, and he certainly did not settle it.

However, Juan Ponce de León is an important figure in history. In a short time, he became one of the richest and most powerful men in the Americas. He established the first city in what is now Puerto Rico and has another city there named after him. And he helped Spain claim valuable lands in the Americas.

A statue of Ponce de León in San Juan,
the capital of Puerto Rico

Ponce de León is remembered for another reason as well. He is the man who led the attacks on three groups of native peoples—the Hispaniola Taino, the Borinquen Taino, and the Caribs—and was responsible for destroying them.

The words on his gravestone fit his place in history. They are:

> "Here rest the bones of a lion
> Mightier in deeds than in name."

# Other Events of the 16th Century
## *(1501 – 1600)*

During the century that Ponce de León was exploring, events were happening in other parts of the world. Some of these were:

**1502**        Portuguese navigator Vasco da Gama makes his second voyage to India in order to expand trade.

**1519**        Hernán Cortés reaches Mexico and by 1521 conquers the Aztecs.

**1520**        Ferdinand Magellan, the Portuguese navigator, sails around the southern tip of South America.

**1524**        Giovanni da Verrazano, an Italian sailor, explores the coast of North America from North Carolina to Maine.

**1534**        Francisco Pizarro of Spain conquers the Inca Empire in Peru.

**1541**        John Calvin spreads Protestantism in France.

# Time Line

**1474?**        Juan Ponce de León is born
in Santervás de Campos,
Spain.

**148?**        Ponce de León works as a page
for Don Pedro Núñez de Guzman.

**149?**        Ponce de León goes off to fight
the Moors.

**1492**        The war with the Moors ends.

**1492**        Columbus returns with news of
uncharted lands.

**1493**        Columbus takes Ponce de León and
2,000 others on his second voyage to
the Americas.

**1493–
1502**        Ponce de León fights against the
Taino. He marries and settles on a
farm on Hispaniola.

**1502**    Ponce de León is put in charge of all military forces on the eastern half of the island.

**1504**    Ponce de León leads Spanish forces into Higuey. He is named deputy governor of that area.

**1506**    Ponce de León leads the Spanish forces going to Borinquen.

**1512**    Diego Columbus wins the right to be governor of Borinquen. Ponce de León begins to look for the island of Bimini. He comes to Florida and discovers the Gulf Stream.

**1521**    Ponce de León sets off on his second expedition to Florida, to settle it. In July he dies of an infected arrow wound.

# Glossary

**Alaminos, Antonio de** (uhl-uh-MEE-nos, an-TOW-nee-oh) The captain of one of the three ships who accompanied Ponce de León on his search for Bimini

**Arawak** (AH-rah-wahk) The large group of native people who lived in the West Indies and eventually were killed off after the Spanish came to the Americas

**Bimini** (BIH-mih-nee) The island in the Caribbean rumored to be the site of the Fountain of Youth

**Borinquen** (bore-in-KEN) The original name for the island of Puerto Rico

**caravels** (KAR-uh-vels) Small, fast sailing ships that were able to carry a lot of men and supplies

**Caribs** (KAR-ubs) Native people who lived near the islands of Borinquen and Hispaniola

**continent** (KAHNT-un-unt) A very large area of land

**current** (KUR-unt) A stream of water that flows very fast and strong

**Fountain of Youth** (FOWN-ten) Magical waters that were believed to cure illnesses and restore youth to all who drank them

**governor** (GUHV-ur-nur) The person who rules an area of land

**Gulf Stream** A strong ocean current that flows northward up the east coast of North America and then across the Atlantic Ocean

**Higuey** (ee-GWAY) The eastern part of the island of Hispaniola. Today it is known as the Dominican Republic.

**Hispaniola** (his-pan-YOW-luh) The first island in the Americas to be settled. It is now the two countries of Haiti and the Dominican Republic.

**Moors** Muslims from North Africa who settled in Spain and were eventually pushed out by the Spanish in 1492

**settlement** A group of people who have left one place to live in another

**Taino** (TEE-now) The native people of Hispaniola

# Index